D0209803

OUTDOOR LIFE

essential

CAMPING

for teens

Kristine Hooks

HIGH
interest
books

Children's Press
A Division of Grolier Publishing
New York / London / Hong Kong / Sydney
Danbury, Connecticut

To my dad, John Hooks, who took me on my first camping trips and taught me to always be calm and resourceful

Book Design: Lisa Quattlebaum
Contributing Editor: Jennifer Ceaser

Photo Credits: p. 5 © Christian Michaels/FPG; pp. 6, 17 (both), 18, 24 © IndexStock; p. 11 © Tim Wright/Corbis; p. 12 © SuperStock; pp. 15, 28, 36, 38 © Laz Burke; p. 22 (both) © Corbis; p. 26 © VCG/FPG; p. 34 © Heath Robbins/FPG.

Visit Children's Press on the Internet at:
http://publishing.grolier.com

Library of Congress Cataloging-in-Publication Data

Hooks, Kristine.
  Essential camping for teens / by Kristine Hooks.
    p. cm.—(Outdoor life)
  Includes bibliographical references (p.) and index.
  Summary: Provides information on where to camp, how to set up a campsite, keeping warm and dry, preparing food while camping, and how to handle emergencies in order to make camping safe, comfortable, and fun.
    ISBN 0-516-23353-x (lib. bdg.) —ISBN 0-516-23553-2 (pbk.)
    1. Camping—Juvenile literature. [1. Camping.] I Title. II. Outdoor life (Children's Press)

GV191.7 .H66 2000
796.5'4—dc21
                                                        99-058216

CONTENTS

Introduction

What is camping? Basically, camping is living outdoors. You set up a temporary shelter and stay outside for at least one night. Camping is a wonderful way to experience nature. It gets you out of your house and into the great outdoors.

The most basic activities of camping are sleeping and eating. A camping trip may also include activities such as hiking, canoeing, biking, and studying nature and wildlife.

Whether you are camping for only one night or for many nights, you need to be prepared. If you've never gone camping, you may have several questions. Where will I camp? With whom will I go camping? How do I set up a camp? How will I stay warm and dry sleeping outside? What will I eat and how will I cook it? How do I build a campfire?

What will I do in case of emergency?

This book will help you answer these questions. You will learn basic information about camping so that all of your trips will be comfortable, fun, and safe.

1
Camping: An Overview

There are two major types of camping: camp-ground camping (also called car camping) and backwoods camping.

CAMPGROUND CAMPING

At campgrounds, campers pay a small fee, about $10 to $20 per night. The fee pays for the upkeep of the campground. Campers are assigned their own campsite. The campsites usually have a picnic table and a fire pit for cooking. Campers can drive directly to their campsite and park there. This means that you can carry whatever supplies you need in your car. Campgrounds usually provide drinking water, bathrooms with showers, and often a small store selling food and supplies. Some campgrounds also have pools or lakes for swimming. There may be game rooms and nightly group activities, such as sing-alongs or

Camping Tip

If you want to camp during the busy summer months, it's a good idea to make a reservation at a campground. Don't forget to ask what facilities the campground offers.

outdoor movies.

People choose to stay at campgrounds for many different reasons. Some want to experience camping and the great outdoors, but they also want modern conveniences, such as bathrooms, showers, and running water. Other campers are vacationers who do not want to pay a lot of money for a hotel. Camping in a campground can be a very inexpensive and fun way for a family to go on vacation.

BACKWOODS CAMPING

Backwoods camping is sometimes referred to as "roughing it." Backwoods camping is an activity for experienced campers who really want to explore nature. Backwoods campers often combine camping with another activity, such as hiking or canoeing. They usually camp for several days or weeks and stay at a different spot every night. Backwoods campers will not have access to the conveniences that most campgrounds provide. They must carry all of their supplies and camping gear with them. Backwoods camping requires a lot of extra care, planning, and safety measures.

You should go backwoods camping with at least one other person. Camping with another person or a group makes it easier to set up camp. It also is the safest way to camp. Also, if an injury or emergency occurs, there is a person who can perform first aid and get help. To learn how to perform basic first aid, check out the Boy Scouts Web site at *www.bsa.scouting.org.*

LEARNING CAMPING SKILLS

Many of the skills you need to know to be a successful camper you can learn on your own. It is a good idea to get some basic camping experience before trying any kind of camping.

Camping Tip

Never go on a backwoods trip without a good topographical (land) map and a compass. Of course, you must know how to read them. Consider taking a course on orienteering. Orienteering will help you know where you are at all times.

Find a book that details everything you need to know about camping. Go with your family or group to a campground. Practice pitching (setting up) a tent in your backyard. Learn how to make and extinguish (put out) a campfire. (See the Smokey the Bear Web site at *www.smokeybear.com* for tips on how to build and extinguish a campfire properly.) Go with a guided group on a short backwoods

Becoming a member of the Boy Scouts is a good way
to learn camping basics.

camping trip. It's important to take small
steps to learn camping basics.

You can also take classes offered by a camping organization. Joining an organization,
such as the Boy Scouts or Girl Scouts, is one
way to get involved. There are also local club
and national associations that you can join.
These include the National Campers and
Hikers Association and the North American
Family Campers Association.

2
Camping Basics

What you need for your camping trip depends on whether you are going car camping or backwoods camping. You need to pack only as much as you can carry if you are backwoods camping. Also, check the weather forecast for the area where you are camping. If it gets much colder at night, you'll need warm sleeping clothes and extra blankets. Don't forget about the possibility of rain. Always carry some basic rain gear just in case!

GEAR AND EQUIPMENT

The most basic camping gear that you'll need is a tent, sleeping bag, cooking equipment and utensils, a lantern or flashlights with extra batteries, and a good knife. You will probably want some type of camp stove, too. A stove will come in handy if weather conditions make it difficult to build a fire.

Camping Tip

Before each camping trip, make a checklist of all the items you will need. Check off each item as you pack it so you won't forget anything.

If you don't have your own camping equipment, ask to borrow some from a friend or family member. You also can find stores that rent equipment. If you become a regular camper, try to invest in the best equipment you can afford. Good camping supplies should last for years.

How do you know which equipment is the best? It is not necessarily the fanciest or the most expensive. A good way to find out what you should buy is by talking to an expert. Visit a local camping supply store and do some investigating. If you don't know what an item is for, just ask! Look at all of the different types of camping equipment the store offers. Find out what the good and bad points are of each

There are different types of tents, such as a dome shape (top) or an A-frame (bottom).

type of equipment. For example, there are seven kinds of camp stoves—each burns a different type of fuel.

Tents

Tents are one case in which bigger is better. After all, your tent is your home away from home, and you want to be comfortable.

Modern tents usually are made of nylon. They come in many different shapes, such as tunnels, domes, and A-frames. Tents are also made to be waterproof, but they may also have additional wind and weather protection.

Your tent should not be too heavy to carry. Backwoods campers should get a tent that weighs less than 12 pounds (5½ kg). Buy a ground tarp (a sheet of waterproof material) to be placed on the floor inside the tent. A tarp will keep moisture from seeping in from the ground while you're sleeping. Be sure that the tent poles and stakes (used to hold the tent in the ground) are made of aluminum, not plastic. Plastic can break easily.

Before your first trip, set up your tent to make sure you have all the necessary parts. Find a grassy area (such as a backyard or a nearby park) where you can practice pitching the tent.

Two examples of mummy-style sleeping bags

Sleeping Bags and Sleeping Pads

Sleeping bags filled with goose down (goose feathers) are the warmest and longest-lasting type of bag. However, they are also the most expensive. Bags filled with synthetic (man-made) materials are much less expensive and will work just as well for most weather conditions. They are priced from about $25 to $100. There are also different styles of sleeping bags. A square style will give you more room to move around. A mummy-style bag will keep

you a little more snug and warm.

With just a sleeping bag and the tent floor between you and the ground, you will feel every rock and stick. A foam pad or an air mattress can be put underneath your sleeping bag. You will be able to sleep much more comfortably.

Clothing

You don't need special clothes for camping, but there are a few basic rules that apply to all outdoor activities:

- Wear clothes in layers. It's easier to adjust to temperatures if you have several layers that you can take off and put on again.
- Do not wear all-cotton clothes next to your skin. If you get wet (from the rain or from sweating), the cotton will trap the moisture. This will make it difficult for your skin to dry off and warm

Wearing nylon material, such as a windbreaker, will help to protect you from the wind.

up. Clothes made out of polyester, silk, wool, or polypropylene (a man-made material) are a better choice. These fabrics allow moisture to evaporate while keeping you warm and dry.

- Always have a winter hat with you. By covering your head, you keep in body heat. If it's going to be cold overnight, wear your hat to bed.
- Wear a nylon or nylon-shell jacket to protect you from the wind.
- Carry rain gear on all of your camping trips, even if it is sunny. The weather can change in an instant. A pair of waterproof pants and a windbreaker or rain poncho work well.
- Your shoes or boots should be comfortable and as light as possible. Wear two pairs of socks made from wool or polypropylene. Turn the pair of socks next to your feet inside out. (The seams

should face away from your feet.) This will help prevent blisters.

- Wear the right kind of clothing to prevent discomfort and possible hypothermia. Hypothermia happens when your body is exposed to wind, wetness, and cold temperatures. A person's body begins to lose heat faster than the heat can be replaced. The temperature of the body begins to drop. A person begins to shiver, lose concentration, and breathe more slowly. If you begin experiencing any of these symptoms, get to someplace warm as soon as possible.

Camping Tip

A large, heavy-duty plastic trash bag makes a good rain poncho. Cut a slit in the bottom of the bag that is big enough to fit your head through. Then cut slits in each side for your arms.

Two styles of packs

Packs

You may not need a pack if you're staying in a campground, but you must have one for backwoods camping. The size of the pack depends on how long your trip will be and on the weather. The colder the weather, the more room you'll need for heavier, thicker clothing.

The heaviest part of your pack should be close to your back and as high as possible. Packing correctly will help protect your back and keep the load balanced. First, waterproof your pack by lining it with a large plastic bag. Put the sleeping gear at the bottom of the pack. Clothing should be packed in the middle. Food, cooking supplies, and the tent should go on top.

Water

You can live for several days without food, but you need water to survive. Access to drinkable water is a necessary part of any camping trip. You need water for drinking, cooking, and washing your cooking equipment. Drinking water is especially important in the summer months. High temperatures and the hot sun can leave you dehydrated. Dehydration occurs when your body doesn't have enough water.

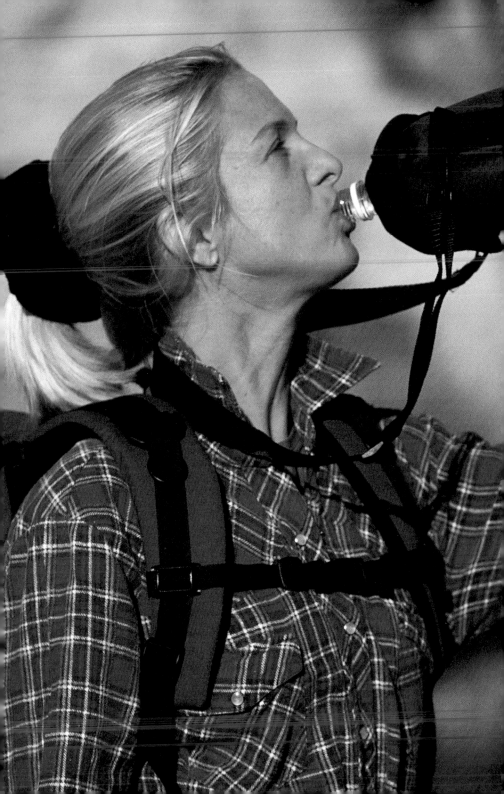

If you are going camping at a camp-ground, you will probably have access to drinking water. Bring a couple of extra jugs of water in the car with you just in case. If you are going backwoods camping, you won't be able to carry much water with you. Each gallon of water weighs 8 pounds. Before you go on a backwoods trip, be sure that there is a water source (a stream or a lake) in the area. ALWAYS boil collected water for five to ten minutes before drinking it or using it for cooking or cleaning! Boiling the water kills bacteria and other things in the water that could make you sick. You may want to buy a water filter system that is small enough to carry. There are also chemical tablets avail-able that will make water drinkable.

It is essential to have access to clean drinking water on your camping trip.

3
Choosing a Campsite

Picking a site to set up camp is very important. It is necessary to take time to choose a site for your own safety. You also should look for a site where you will do the least amount of damage to the environment.

IN THE CAMPGROUND

If you're staying at a campground, you can drive around and inspect a few sites before you choose one. Pick a site that provides the most level (flat) ground surface for your tent. Make sure that an area is big enough to set up your tent. Determine how far away the bathrooms are and how close other campers are—you may not mind being far away from the bathroom if you have more privacy.

IN THE WOODS

As with campground camping, in the woods

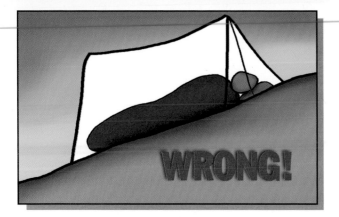

Be sure to position your sleeping bag to lie side to side (top) instead of head to toe (bottom).

you want to choose as flat a campsite as possible. Sleeping on an incline (slanted ground) can be very uncomfortable. There are times when you may have to set up on an incline, such as the side of a mountain. Position your sleeping bag so that you lie side to side, not from head to toe (or toe to head). You should use extra clothing and padding to raise up the lower side of your sleeping bag so that it is as level as possible.

Camping Tip

Never bring a lit lantern into a tent. Lanterns give off carbon monoxide (CO). CO is a dangerous and potentially deadly gas.

Pick either a designated campsite or find a place where others have camped. Designated sites should be marked on your topographical map. The reason for choosing a site that has already been used is that camping damages the land. Grass is trampled and campfires leave burned holes in the ground. Choosing sites where people have camped contains the damaged areas. These sites may also provide benefits for you. Water sources may be nearby. Holes for toilets may already be dug. There may even be simple shelters built for added protection from the weather.

Following these rules will help reduce the wear-and-tear on the environment. Doing your part will keep the outdoors beautiful for future generations.

1. Travel and camp in designated areas. Stay on marked trails so you don't trample plants or animals.
2. Dispose of waste properly. "Pack out what you pack in!" Bring extra garbage bags with you to bag up trash and carry it out of the park.
3. Leave what you find. Leave your campsite and the trail in the same condition as you found them. Of course, if you find trash along the trail, pick it up and take it back out with you!
4. Minimize campfire impact. Try to build

fires only in designated fire pits or fire rings. (These are usually made out of rocks.) Otherwise, find a place that was recently used for a campfire. (You should see a blackened patch of land.)

5. Respect wildlife. For your own safety and the safety of the animals, keep your distance from them. Don't attract wildlife to your campsite by leaving out food or trash. Also, keep in mind that animals live in the woods. Don't do things to destroy their habitat. Don't pollute rivers, streams, and lakes with soap or human waste. Don't harm the plants and trees, which they use for food and to build their homes. Don't feed animals human food. Keep your noise level down so you don't scare or disturb wildlife.

6. Be considerate. Don't talk or play music so loudly that you bother other campers. Always be helpful and courteous to other campers.

Beware of Bears

Bears are attracted to campsites by smells. These smells include food, deodorants, and perfumes. Never store food in your tent. Avoid wearing sweet-smelling perfumes. If your clothes have food smells on them, leave them outside and wear something else to bed.

Always keep your food as far from your tent as possible. Double-bag all food containers and hang the bags in a tree, about 10 feet (3 m) above the ground. Some campgrounds provide steel boxes for storing food.

If you encounter a bear in your campsite, many people suggest banging some pots and pans together to scare the bear off. If the bear is moving toward you, back away slowly, talking in a firm, loud voice and waving your arms high above your head. DON'T RUN!

SETTING UP CAMP SAFELY

Keep in mind these safety issues when choosing a campsite in the woods.

- Don't choose a site that is too close to water. You should be no closer than 200 feet (60 m). Wild animals, such as bears and cougars, use the water, too.
- Don't set up your tent under a rotted or dying tree or one with dead branches.
- Don't camp in a flat, open meadow where your tent is the tallest thing in the area. Lightning usually strikes the tallest object in its path to the ground. Remember that your tent poles and stakes are made of metal, which attracts lightning.
- Never set up your sleeping space in a depression, or ditch, in the ground. If rain falls during night, it can fill up the hole, leaving you very wet.

4
Eating Out

At the end of a day filled with hiking, swimming, or canoeing, you will probably want a good, hot meal. Even backwoods campers, who don't have coolers or a lot of kitchen utensils, can still have a hot meal.

FOOD

Freeze-dried meals, also called MREs (Meals Ready to Eat), are packaged in plastic pouches. They do not need refrigeration and can be eaten after soaking in boiling water. They come in many different selections, including stew, lasagna, and pasta. Another option is pre-mixed pasta and rice dishes, which can make a simple, one-pot meal.

All campers should take foods with them that are easy to carry and that don't need to be refrigerated. Apples, oranges, bananas, nuts, and energy bars are good choices. When the

Campstoves come in many different styles, including two-burner (top) and single-burner (bottom) types.

weather is cool, you can even carry hard cheeses and cured meats, such as pepperoni.

CAMP STOVES

It's a good idea to have a camp stove with you on every camping trip. It is almost impossible to start a fire with wet firewood. There are many different types of camp stoves, but the most popular use gasoline, propane, butane, or kerosene fuels. The stoves come in different

- Sprained ankles can be avoided by wearing good fitting shoes with strong ankle support.
- If serious injuries occur, send one person in your camping party for help. Have one person stay with the injured person.

Important Camping Tips

- Know how to build a campfire. Always be sure that your campfire is completely extinguished.
- Never bring a lit lantern into a tent.
- Always dress sensibly and for any kind of weather.
- Learn how to read maps and a compass.
- Act in a mature and safe manner at all times. Be aware of your environment.

NEW WORDS

backwoods wooded or partly cleared areas far from cities

camp (noun) a ground on which temporary shelters (such as tents) are set up; (verb) to live temporarily outdoors

campground area that is set aside for camping that often has modern conveniences

campsite area where a camp is set up

carbon monoxide a poisonous gas that has no color or odor

compass a device for determining direction (north, south, east, or west)

dehydration loss of water and bodily fluids

depression an area that is not level with the ground around it, a ditch

extinguish put out, as in a fire

fire pit (also called fire ring) area set aside for having campfires; it is usually a circle of rocks

hypothermia a dangerous condition in which one's body temperature is well below normal

incline on a slant

kindling sticks and small branches used to build a fire

MREs Meals Ready to Eat; freeze-dried meals

orienteering to orient oneself, or become familiar with one's position

pitch to set up a tent

polypropylene manmade fabric

poncho loose rain clothing that is often made of plastic

stake sharp metal sticks used to hold a tent in the ground

synthetic manmade

tarp sheet of waterproof material

tent a portable shelter made of fabric, such as nylon or canvas

tinder dry material, such as small twigs and tree bard, that catches fire quickly

topographical map map showing distances, elevations, rivers, lakes, mountains, and other natural and man-made features of an area

FOR FURTHER READING

Books

Jacobson, Cliff. *Basic Essentials*™ *Camping (2nd Edition)*. Old Saybrook, CT: The Globe Pequot Press, 1999.

McManners, Hugh. *The Backpacker's Handbook*. New York: DK, 1995.

Rutter, Michael. *Camping Made Easy: A Manual for Beginners with Tips for the Experienced*. Old Saybrook, CT: The Globe Pequot Press, 1997.

Magazine

Outdoor Explorer
2 Park Avenue, 10th Floor
New York, NY 10016
(800) 365-1978
Web site: *www.outdoorexplorer.com*

RESOURCES

About.com Guide to Camping

http://camping.about.com/travel/camping
Presents a variety of articles and information sources about camping.

Absolute Authority on Wilderness Camping

www.absoluteauthority.com
Under *Search*, enter "Wilderness Camping."
An experienced camper fills this site with news and articles about camping, information on education and training programs, and links to products and services.

Boy Scouts of America and Girl Scouts of America

www.bsa.scouting.org
www.gsusa.org
To find out if there is an active scouting troop in your neighborhood, look in the phone directory under "Boy Scouts" or "Girl Scouts."

L.L. Bean

www.llbean.com

Sells outdoor clothing and also offers a park search and an "Outdoors Online" feature for expert advice on outdoor sports.

National Park Service

www.nps.gov

Includes general information about campgrounds in the National Forest system. There are guides to natural resources in national parks, as well as historical information.

INDEX

About the Author

Kristine Hooks is a lawyer living in New York City. Kristine has enjoyed camping ever since she was a Girl Scout. Recently, she has camped in Yosemite and Yellowstone National Parks.